Informing the legislative debate since 1914

Asylum and Gang Violence: Legal Overview

Kate M. Manuel
Legislative Attorney

September 5, 2014

Congressional Research Service

7-5700

www.crs.gov

R43716

Summary

The recent increase in the number of unaccompanied alien children (UACs) apprehended at the border between Mexico and the United States has raised questions about the role that gang-related violence in Central America may play in determining whether such children are eligible for refugee status and asylum. Only aliens who are "refugees," as that term is defined by the Immigration and Nationality Act (INA), qualify for potential refugee status or asylum (two forms of discretionary relief that could enable UACs to enter or remain in the United States).

The INA's definition, in turn, generally encompasses individuals outside their home country who are unable or unwilling to return to that country because of "persecution or a well-founded fear of persecution on account of race, religion, nationality, membership in a particular social group, or political opinion." However, key terms within this definition—including *persecution* and *particular social group*—are not defined by statute or regulation. Instead, they have been construed by the Board of Immigration Appeals (BIA), the highest administrative tribunal for interpreting and applying immigration law, through a process of case-by-case adjudication, with the federal courts generally deferring to the BIA's interpretation insofar as it is based on a "permissible construction" of the INA. These cases center upon eligibility for asylum, because denials of applications for refugee status cannot be appealed. Denials of asylum by immigration judges in the course of formal removal proceedings, in contrast, may be appealed to the BIA and the federal courts of appeals.

Persecution has been construed to mean the infliction of harm by the government, or an entity the government is unable or unwilling to control, "upon persons who differ in a way regarded as offensive ..., in a manner condemned by civilized governments." A showing of past persecution establishes a rebuttable presumption that the alien has a well-founded fear of future persecution. Otherwise, aliens must prove they subjectively fear persecution, and there is a "reasonable possibility" they would suffer persecution if returned to their home country. Such a "reasonable possibility" can exist when there is less than a 50% chance of the occurrence taking place. This persecution must also be "on account of" a protected ground (e.g., race). The REAL ID Act of 2005 (P.L. 109-13) amended the INA to require that a protected ground "was or will be at least one central reason" for the persecution. However, *central reason* has been construed to mean a reason that is more than "incidental, tangential, superficial, or subordinate to another reason," not as the only or primary reason. Most protected grounds (i.e., race, religion, nationality, political opinion) are fairly straightforward in their definition, if not in their application in specific cases. *Particular social group*, however, has been construed in various ways by the BIA over the years.

When considered by the BIA or appellate courts in light of how the INA's definition of *refugee* is construed, claims to asylum based on gang-related violence frequently (although not inevitably) fail. In some cases, this is because the harm experienced or feared by the alien is seen not as persecution, but as generalized lawlessness or criminal activity. In other cases, persecution has been found to be lacking because governmental ineffectiveness in controlling the gangs is distinguished from inability or unwillingness to control them. In yet other cases, any persecution that is found is seen as lacking the requisite connection to a protected ground, and instead arising from activities "typical" to gangs, such as extortion and recruitment of new members. The particular social group articulated by the alien (e.g., former gang members, recruits) may also been seen as lacking a "common, immutable characteristic," social visibility (now, social distinction), or particularity.

Contents

Contacts

T he recent increase in the number of unaccompanied alien children (UACs) apprehended at the border between Mexico and the United States has raised questions about the role that gang-related violence in Central America may play in determining eligibility for refugee status and asylum.[1] Gang activity is wide-spread in El Salvador, Guatemala, and Honduras,[2] and attempts by these governments to control such activity have been seen as ineffective, at best, or as violating the civil rights of persons perceived as gang members or associates, at worst.[3] The Office of the United Nations High Commissioner for Refugees (UNHCR) repeatedly noted this gang-related violence in its 2014 report, *Children on the Run: Unaccompanied Children Leaving Central America and Mexico and the Need for International Protection.*[4] Subsequently, in discussing the "surge" in the number of UACs arriving at the U.S.-Mexican border in FY2014, the UNHRC reiterated that 58% of these children cite "violence" in their home countries as "at least one key reason" for leaving.[5]

Refugee status and asylum are two forms of discretionary relief that could enable UACs to enter or remain in the United States, and the Immigration and Nationality Act (INA) relies upon the same definition in determining eligibility for both.[6] In both cases, to be eligible, aliens must prove that they have experienced past persecution, or have a well-founded fear of future persecution, on account of race, religion, nationality, political opinion, or membership in a particular social group.[7] However, refugee status may only be granted to aliens outside the United States, while asylum may only be granted to aliens arriving at a port of entry or the U.S. border, or within the United States.[8] Applicants for refugee status are also barred from appealing denials of their applications, while applicants for asylum are not.[9] Thus, an equivalent to the extensive body of case law construing and applying the INA's definition of *refugee* in the context of asylum is lacking in the context of refugee status. Instead, the meaning of *refugee* for purposes of refugee status is typically construed in light of asylum cases, and asylum is the focus of this report.

---

[1] *See, e.g.*, Richard Cowan, *Calls in U.S. Congress for Refugee Status for Central American Kids*, Reuters, June 27, 2014, *available at* http://www.reuters.com/article/2014/06/27/us-usa-immigration-children-idUSKBN0F229L20140627; Julia Preston, *Rush to Deport Young Migrants Could Trample Asylum Claims*, N.Y. Times, July 19, 2014, *available at* http://www nytimes.com/2014/07/20/us/rush-to-deport-young-migrants-could-trample-asylum-claims- html. For more on UACs, including the legal definition of an *unaccompanied alien child*, see CRS Report R43623, *Unaccompanied Alien Children—Legal Issues: Answers to Frequently Asked Questions*, by Kate M. Manuel and Michael John Garcia. For additional background on UACs, see CRS Report R43599, *Unaccompanied Alien Children: An Overview*, by Lisa Seghetti, Alison Siskin, and Ruth Ellen Wasem.

[2] *See generally* CRS Report RL34112, *Gangs in Central America*, by Clare Ribando Seelke.

[3] *See, e.g.*, Washington Office on Latin America (WOLA), Central American Gang-Related Asylum: A Resource Guide, May 2008, at 4-5, *available at* http://www.wola.org/sites/default/files/downloadable/Central%20America/past/CA%20Gang-Related%20Asylum.pdf; Alexandra M. Gonçalves-Peña, *Challenging the "Political": U.S. Asylum Law and Central American Gang Warfare*, 65 GUILD PRAC. 242, 243 (2008).

[4] This report is available at http://www.unhcrwashington.org/sites/default/files/1_UAC_Children%20on%20the%20Run_Full%20Report.pdf (last accessed: Aug. 12, 2014).

[5] Jana Mason, Senior Advisor for U.S. Government Relations, UNHCR, Testimony before the Senate Committee on Appropriations, July 10, 2014, at 2, *available at* http://www.appropriations.senate.gov/sites/default/files/hearings/UNHCR%20Statement%20UAC.7.10.14.FINAL_.pdf.

[6] *See* INA §207(a)(2), 8 U.S.C. §1157(a)(2) (refugee status); INA §208(b)(1)(A), 8 U.S.C. §1158(b)(1)(A) (asylum). The INA is codified in Title 8 of the United States Code, and references to it in this report also include references to the corresponding sections of Title 8. However, Title 8 also includes provisions that are not part of the INA. Citations to such provisions will have no corresponding citation to the INA.

[7] INA §101(a)(42), 8 U.S.C. §1101(a)(42).

[8] *Compare* INA §207(b), 8 U.S.C. §1157(b) (refugee status); INA §208(a)(1), 8 U.S.C. §1158(a)(1) (asylum).

[9] *Compare* INA §242(a)(2)(B)(ii), 8 U.S.C. §1252(a)(2)(B)(ii) (asylum) *with* 8 C.F.R. §207.3(b) (refugee status).

The report provides an overview of the basis for asylum in U.S. law. It also discusses how key elements of the INA's definition of *refugee* have been construed and applied in gang-related asylum cases. The report briefly notes, in relevant places, related forms of relief from removal, such as withholding of removal under Section 241 of the INA or the Convention against Torture and Other Cruel, Inhuman, or Degrading Treatment or Punishment, but does not provide a comprehensive treatment of these topics.

It is also important to note that many potentially relevant decisions—namely, those by asylum officers within U.S. Citizenship and Immigration Services (USCIS) and immigration judges within the Executive Office for Immigration Review (EOIR) at the Department of Justice (DOJ)—are not published. There are reasons to believe that USCIS and EOIR may be more receptive to gang-related asylum claims than the decisions by the Board of Immigration Appeals (BIA) and the federal courts of appeals discussed here.[10] However, USCIS and immigration judge decisions are not publicly available in the same way that published BIA decisions and federal court decisions are.

USCIS or Immigration Judges: Who Has Jurisdiction over Which Asylum Claims?

USCIS generally hears only so-called *affirmative applications* for asylum, or applications made by aliens who are not in removal proceedings. However, the William Wilberforce Trafficking Victims Protection Reauthorization Act (TVPRA) of 2008 (P.L. 110-457) amended the INA to provide that USCIS has "initial jurisdiction" over all applications for asylum filed by UACs, regardless of whether the UAC has been placed in removal proceedings. With the exception of applications by UACs, immigration judges within EOIR hear all *defensive applications* for asylum, or applications made by aliens in removal proceedings.

If an asylum officer denies the alien's application and the alien has a legal immigration status at the time of the denial, the alien remains in that status. However, if the alien is not in a legal immigration status at the time of the denial, he or she is placed in removal proceedings, and the application is reviewed *de novo* by an immigration judge in the course of removal proceedings.

The immigration judge's decision may be appealed to the BIA by either the alien (in the case of denials) or the government (in cases where asylum is granted). The BIA's decision, in turn, may be appealed by the alien to the federal courts of appeals. The government may not appeal BIA decisions to the appellate courts, but BIA decisions may be certified to the Attorney General, who can overturn them.

See generally 8 C.F.R. Part 208, Subpart A (asylum procedures); 8 C.F.R. §1003.1(h)(1)(i)-(iii) (certification of BIA decisions to the Attorney General).

Basis for Asylum in International and U.S. Law

The INA's current protections for refugees and asylees are grounded in the 1951 Convention Relating to the Status of Refugees and the 1967 Protocol Relating to the Status of Refugees.[11] The Convention generally defined a *refugee* as any person who

> [a]s a result of events occurring before 1 January 1951 and owing to well-founded fear of being persecuted for reasons of race, religion, nationality, membership of a particular social

---

[10] *See, e.g.*, Matthew J. Lister, *Gang-Related Asylum Claims: An Overview and Prescription*, 38 U. MEM. L. REV. 727, 736 (2008) (noting a case wherein the immigration judge found that abandoned street children constituted a cognizable social group); Michele A. Voss, *Young and Marked for Death: Expanding the Definition of Particular Social Group in Asylum Law to Include Youth Victims of Gang Persecution*, 37 RUTGERS L.J. 235, 272 (2005) (noting a case wherein the immigration judge granted asylum to an alien who had been "heavily recruited" by a gang).

[11] Prior to being amended to reflect the protections of Convention and Protocol, the INA had its own provisions as to the treatment of refugees. *See, e.g.*, INA §203(a)(7)(A)(i), 8 U.S.C. §1153(a)(7)(A)(i) (1976) (providing that "conditional entry" could be granted to aliens from a Communist-dominated area or from the Middle East who feared persecution on account of race, religion, or political opinion).

group, or political opinion, is outside the country of his nationality and is unable or, owing to such fear, is unwilling to avail himself of the protection of that country,[12]

although persons who had "committed a crime against peace, a war crime, or a crime against humanity" were expressly excluded from this definition.[13] Most notably, the Convention barred nations which are parties to it from returning refugees to their home country (or another country) where they feared persecution.[14] It also obligated these nations to grant refugees freedom of religion and movement, the right to work and public education, and access to identity papers and travel documents, among other things.[15] Conversely, it required refugees to respect the laws and regulations of their country of asylum.[16] The United States was involved in drafting the Convention, but did not sign on as a party to it.[17] However, it did sign on as a party to the Protocol, which amended the Convention by removing the temporal restrictions (i.e., "events occurring before 1 January 1951") from its definition of *refugee*.[18]

The Refugee Act of 1980 (P.L. 96-212) is widely recognized as having been enacted to bring U.S. domestic law into conformity with the United States' commitments under the Protocol.[19] Among other things, the Refugee Act amended Section 101(a)(42) of the INA to define *refugee* in largely the same terms used by the Convention and Protocol:

> The term "refugee" means ... any person who is outside any country of such person's nationality or, in the case of a person having no nationality, is outside any country in which such person last habitually resided, and who is unable or unwilling to return to, and is unable or unwilling to avail himself or herself of the protection of, that country because of persecution or a well-founded fear of persecution on account of race, religion, nationality, membership in a particular social group, or political opinion.[20]

The Refugee Act also added the current Sections 207, 208, and 209 to the INA, which, respectively, address refugee admissions, the granting of asylum, and the adjustment of refugees' and asylees' status to that of lawfully permanent resident aliens (LPRs).[21] In addition, the Refugee

---

[12] 1951 Convention Relating to the Status of Refugees, 189 U.N. TREATY SERIES 137 (entered into force Apr. 22, 1954), at Art. 1A(2).

[13] *Id*. at Art. 1F.

[14] *Id*. at Art. 33. This restriction is commonly referred to as the prohibition upon *refoulement*, using the French term for "return." *But see* Sale v. Haitian Centers Council, Inc., 509 U.S. 155 (1993) (debating the best translation of "refoulement" into English).

[15] Convention Relating to the Status of Refugees, *supra* note 12, at Art. 4 (religion), Art. 17 (work), Art. 22 (public education), Art. 26 (movement), Art. 27 (identity papers), Art. 28 (travel documents).

[16] *Id*. at Art. 2 ("Every refugee has duties to the country in which he finds himself, which require that he conform to its laws and regulations as well as to measures taken for the maintenance of public order.").

[17] *See, e.g.*, Lorena S. Rivas-Tiemann, *Asylum to a Particular Social Group: New Developments and Its Future for Gang-Violence Victims*, 47 TULSA L. REV. 477, 479 (2011) (describing the United States as one of twenty-six countries sending delegates to the meeting that developed the 1951 Convention).

[18] Protocol Relating to the Status of Refugees, 606 U.N. TREATY SERIES 267 (entered into force Oct. 4, 1967). The Protocol adopted Articles 2 to 34 of the Convention, with only slight modifications.

[19] INS v. Cardoza-Fonseca, 480 U.S. 421, 436 (1987) ("If one thing is clear from the legislative history of the new definition of 'refugee,' and indeed the entire 1980 Act, it is that one of Congress' primary purposes was to bring United States refugee law into conformance with the 1967 United Nations Protocol.... ").

[20] P.L. 96-212, §201(a), 94 Stat. 102-103 (Mar. 17, 1980) (codified, as amended, at 8 U.S.C. §1101(a)(42)). This definition also permits "in-country processing" of refugees—or the admission as refugees of aliens who are not outside their country of nationality or last habitual residence—after "appropriate consultation" with Congress. *Id*.

[21] P.L. 96-212, §201(b), 94 Stat. 103-106 (codified, as amended, at 8 U.S.C. §§1157-1159).

Act amended then-Section 243 of the INA to generally bar the return of aliens to countries where the "alien's life or freedom would be threatened ... on account of race, religion, nationality, membership in a particular social group, or political opinion."[22] Subsequently relocated to Section 241 of the INA, this prohibition forms the basis for what is referred to as *withholding of removal*.

Withholding of removal under Section 241 of the INA represents the U.S.'s primary obligation under the Convention and Protocol.[23] That is, as a party to the Protocol, the United States is barred from removing aliens, including aliens arriving at the U.S. border, to a county where he or she would be persecuted.[24] The United States is not required, by the Protocol or otherwise, to admit refugees to the United States, grant asylum to persons in the United States, or permit refugees or asylees to adjust to LPR status or obtain citizenship. To the contrary, the INA expressly notes that the granting of asylum is discretionary,[25] and courts have upheld its denial even when an alien fulfills the requirements of the statutory definition of *refugee*.[26]

Withholding of Removal under the INA & the Convention Against Torture

Aliens seeking **withholding of removal** under Section 241 of the INA face a higher burden of proof than aliens seeking asylum. Such aliens must show that it is "more likely than not" that they would be persecuted if removed, as opposed to showing the well-founded fear of persecution required for asylum. Also unlike asylum, withholding under Section 241 does not provide the alien with a basis to adjust to LPR status or obtain citizenship. Nor does it provide relief for eligible family members in the United States or the ability to petition to bring eligible family members to the United States. Withholding under Section 241 may, however, be available to aliens who are ineligible for asylum, for example, because their claims are time-barred.

The U.N. **Convention Against Torture (CAT)** prohibits the United States from returning a person to a country where he or she would "more likely than not" be tortured, a term which is defined by federal regulations to encompass any act by which pain or suffering is intentionally inflicted by or at the instigation of, or with the consent or acquiescence of, a public official or other person acting in an official capacity for purposes of punishment, intimidation, coercion, or obtaining a confession or other information, or for any discriminatory purpose. The burden of proof for CAT protection is "more likely than not," as with withholding under the INA. However, the alien must show that he or she is more likely than not to be tortured, as opposed to persecuted. Aliens granted CAT protection are also ineligible to adjust to LPR status, obtain citizenship, or bring family members to the United States. CAT protection is, however, available to aliens not afforded other protections (e.g., persecutors, terrorists).

See generally U.S. Department of Justice, EOIR, Asylum and Withholding of Removal Relief, Convention Against Torture Protections: Fact Sheet, Jan. 15, 2009, *available at* http://www.justice.gov/eoir/press/09/AsylumWithholdingCATProtections.pdf.

It is also important to note that, even though the United States signed on as a party to the Protocol, and the INA's definition of *refugee* generally corresponds to that in the Convention and

---

[22] P.L. 96-212, §202(e), 94 Stat. 107 (codified, as amended, at 8 U.S.C. §1231(b)(3)(A)). There are certain exceptions to this prohibition. *See* INA §241(b)(3)(B), 8 U.S.C. §1231(b)(3)(B) (exempting aliens who ordered, incited, assisted, or "otherwise participated in" the persecution of others from the prohibition upon the return of aliens to countries where their life or freedom would be threatened).

[23] *See generally* David A. Martin et al., *Forced Migration Law and Policy* 88-89 (2d ed., 2013).

[24] 1951 Convention Relating to the Status of Refugees, *supra* note 12, at Art. 33.

[25] INA §208(b)(1)(A), 8 U.S.C. §1158(b)(1)(A) ("The Secretary of Homeland Security or the Attorney General *may* grant asylum to an alien.") (emphasis added).

[26] *See, e.g., Cardoza-Fonseca*, 480 U.S. at 443 ("[A]n alien who satisfies the applicable standard under § 208(a) does not have a right to remain in the United States; he or she is simply eligible for asylum, if the Attorney General, in his discretion, chooses to grant it."); *In re* T-Z-, 24 I. & N. Dec. 163 (BIA 2007) (upholding an immigration judge's denial of asylum to an alien who fell within the INA's definition of *refugee*, but had lied to the court).

Protocol, it is U.S. domestic law—not international law—that governs U.S. obligations as to individual aliens.[27] Relatedly, the same terms (e.g., *persecution, particular social group*) may be construed differently when used in the Convention and Protocol than when used in the INA.[28]

Application of the INA's Definition of *Refugee*

Aliens seeking asylum in the United States have the burden of establishing, by a preponderance of the evidence, that they are "refugees" under the INA's definition of this term.[29] This means showing that they (1) have suffered persecution, or (2) have a well-founded fear of persecution (3) on account of (4) a protected ground (i.e., race, religion, nationality, political opinion, or membership in a particular social group). However, the meaning of certain of these terms—such as *persecution* and *particular social group*—is not established by Convention or Protocol, or by the INA and its implementing regulations.[30] Instead, their meaning has been determined by the Board of Immigration Appeals (BIA)—the highest administrative tribunal for interpreting and applying immigration law— through case-by-case adjudication, with the federal courts generally deferring to the BIA's interpretation so long as it is based on a "permissible construction" of the INA.[31] In other cases, such as with the meaning of *well-founded fear*, the executive branch has interpreted particular language within the INA's definition of *refugee* through the promulgation of regulations. These regulatory interpretations are also afforded deference by the courts insofar as they are based on "permissible" constructions of the statutory language. In yet other cases, Congress has enacted legislation that affects how particular terms within the *refugee* definition are construed. Perhaps the most notable example of this is the

> **Consideration of the Alien's Credibility**
>
> Assessments of the alien's credibility by asylum officers and immigration judges can play a significant role in the asylum process. Section 208 of the INA expressly provides that the testimony of the applicant may be sufficient to sustain the applicant's burden of proof in establishing that he or she is a refugee, provided that the applicant satisfies the trier of fact that his or her testimony (1) is credible, (2) is persuasive, and (3) refers to specific facts sufficient to demonstrate that the applicant is a refugee. However, applicants can be found to be credible in their testimony and still be denied asylum (e.g., if the testimony is not persuasive, or does not refer to specific facts demonstrating the applicant is a refugee). Also, as previously noted, grants of asylum are always discretionary.
>
> *See generally* INA §208(b)(1)(B)(ii), 8 U.S.C. §1158(b)(1)(B)(ii); *In re* S-M-J-, 21 I. & N. Dec. 722 (BIA 1997).

---

[27] *See, e.g.,* INS v. Aguirre-Aguirre, 526 U.S. 415, 427 (1999) ("The U. N. Handbook [on the Convention and Protocol] may be a useful interpretative aid, but it is not binding on the Attorney General, the BIA [Board of Immigration Appeals], or United States courts."); *In re* Q-T-M-T-, 21 I. & N. Dec. 639, 649-650 n.5 (similar).

[28] *See infra* notes 101-103 and accompanying text.

[29] *See* INA §208(b)(1)(B)(i), 8 U.S.C. §1158(b)(1)(B)(i); 8 C.F.R. §208.13(a).

[30] The then-Immigration and Naturalization Service (INS) proposed regulations that would have defined key terms related to asylum and withholding in 2000. *See* Dep't of Justice, INS, Asylum and Withholding Definitions: Proposed Rule, 65 Fed. Reg. 76588 (Dec. 7, 2000). However, no such regulations have been finalized to date.

[31] Chevron U.S.A., Inc. v. Natural Resources Defense Council, 467 U.S. 837, 843 (1984). The agency's interpretation need not be the one that the court would have adopted had it interpreted the statute on its own. Rather, the interpretation need only be deemed "reasonable" in order to be upheld. *See, e.g.,* Claros Cantarero v. Holder, 734 F.3d 82, 86 (1st Cir. 2013) ("We cannot say that the BIA's interpretation is either unreasonable or impermissible."); Ulloa Santos v. Attorney General, 552 F. App'x 197, 200 (3d Cir. 2014) ("We ... accord deference to the BIA's interpretation of the INA under the standard established by *Chevron*.").

REAL ID Act of 2005 (P.L. 109-13), which amended the INA to require that a protected ground (e.g., race, religion, nationality) "was or will be at least one central reason" for the persecution.[32]

The application of the INA's definition of *refugee* to aliens seeking asylum in the United States due, in whole or in part, to gang-related violence is, thus, complicated because it involves consideration of an extensive body of statutes, regulations, and administrative and judicial decisions. In addition, the federal courts of appeals can sometimes have differing opinions on whether particular interpretations advanced by the BIA are "permissible" and, thus, entitled to deference.[33] Such differences of opinion can result in aliens' applications for asylum faring differently depending upon the territorial jurisdiction in which they are made (e.g., some courts are willing to consider former gang members as a particular social group, while others are not).[34]

"Persecution"

"Persecution"—or a well-founded fear thereof, discussed below (see "Well-Founded Fear")—underlies international and domestic protections for refugees and asylees. However, neither the Convention and Protocol nor the INA defines *persecution*. Instead, what have been described as the "working parameters of this term"[35] for purposes of U.S. law were established by the BIA in its 1983 decision in *Matter of Laipenieks*. There, the BIA characterized persecution as

> [t]he infliction of suffering or harm, under government sanction, upon persons who differ in a way regarded as offensive (e.g., race, religion, political opinion, etc.), in a manner condemned by civilized governments. The harm or suffering need not be physical, but may take other forms, such as the deliberate imposition of severe economic disadvantage or the deprivation of liberty, food, housing, employment or other essentials of life.[36]

Subsequent decisions built upon this formulation by distinguishing harm that rises to the level of persecution (i.e., harm inflicted "in a manner condemned by civilized governments") from harm that does not, and by clarifying when the actions of private persons can be said to be "under government sanction."

---

[32] *See* P.L. 109-13, div. B, tit. I, §101(a)(3), 119 Stat. 302-303 (May 11, 2005) (codified at 8 U.S.C. §1158(b)(1)(B)(i)).

[33] *Compare* Orellana-Monson v. Holder, 685 F.3d 511, 521 (5th Cir. 2012) ("Contrary to the [alien petitioners'] contention, the BIA's current ... social visibility test is not a radical departure from prior interpretation, but rather a subtle shift that evolved out of the BIA's prior decisions on similar cases and is a reasoned interpretation, which is therefore entitled to deference.") *with* Valdiviezo-Galdamez v. Attorney General, 663 F.3d 582, 603 (3d Cir. 2011) ("Since the 'social visibility' requirement is inconsistent with past BIA decisions, we conclude that it is an unreasonable addition to the requirements for establishing refugee status where that status turns upon persecution on account of membership in a particular social group.").

[34] *Cf.* Jaya Ramji-Nogales, Andrew I. Schoenholtz, & Philip G. Schrag, *Refugee Roulette: Disparities in Asylum Adjudication*, 60 STANFORD L. REV. 295, 302 (2007) ("The statistics that we have collected and analyzed ... suggest that in the world of asylum adjudication, there is remarkable variation in decision making from one official to the next, from one office to the next, from one region to the next, from one Court of Appeals to the next."). It should also be noted that the specific arguments made by the alien, and the evidence he or she produces, also play a significant role in determining the outcome in these cases.

[35] Abdel-Masieh v. U.S. INS, 73 F.3d 579, 583 (5th Cir. 1996).

[36] 18 I. & N. Dec. 433, 456-457 (BIA 1983), *rev'd on other grounds*, 750 F.2d 1427 (9th Cir. 1985). While *Laipenieks* itself distinguished prosecution—or the "punishment of criminal conduct"—from persecution, it noted that "where that punishment entails such things as severe beatings or being sent to a Nazi concentration camp ... and is motivated by one of the specified grounds, such punishment would constitute persecution under the Act." 18 I. & N. Dec. at 459 n.18.

In distinguishing between persecution and other types of harm, the BIA and the courts have contrasted the "extreme" or "serious" nature of the harm that constitutes persecution with harassment, discrimination, and other "lesser" harms that do not rise to the level of persecution.[37] For example, in its 2013 decision in *Martinez-Beltrand v. Attorney General*, the U.S. Court of Appeals for the Third Circuit upheld the denial of asylum to an alien who claimed to have been persecuted by gang members in Honduras on the grounds that the alien had suffered "harassment" that "did not rise to the level of persecution."[38] The alien alleged that she had been persecuted in the past by gang members coming to

> **Forced Recruitment as Persecution?**
>
> The UNHCR has expressed the view that "[f]orcible recruitment attempts, including under death threat, by violent groups would normally amount to persecution." U.S. courts, in contrast, have taken a different approach. The Supreme Court's 1992 decision in *INS v. Elias-Zacarias*, 502 U.S. 478, is generally seen to have foreclosed the argument that forced recruitment—in that case, to a Guatemalan guerilla organization—is *per se* persecution. However, some courts have subsequently suggested that the *Elias-Zacarias* decision does not mean that all claims involving forced recruitment are, *per se*, foreclosed. Rather, these claims are to be considered in light of the facts and circumstances of the case.
>
> *See generally* UNHCR, *Guidance Note on Refugee Claims Relating to Victims of Organized Gangs*, Mar. 31, 2010, at 7-8, *available at* http://www.refworld.org/pdfid/4bb21fa02.pdf ; Rivera-Barrientos v. Holder, 666 F.3d 641, 646 (10th Cir. 2012); In re Vigil, 19 I. & N. Dec. 572, 577-578 (BIA 1988).

the funeral home her family operated, and asking her to give them money and join the gang.[39] Thereafter, gang members allegedly called the funeral home periodically, asking for money.[40] However, the Third Circuit likened these harms to "minor assaults that do not require medical care" or "unfulfilled threats," both of which are generally seen as insufficient to show persecution.[41] It also viewed the gang's actions as "attempt[s] to extort money" and, thus, "ordinary criminal activity" of the sort that "does not rise to the level of persecution necessary to establish eligibility for asylum."[42]

The U.S. Court of Appeals for the Tenth Circuit relied upon similar logic in its 2013 decision in *Cosenza-Cruz v. Holder*, where the extortion attempts and threats experienced by two brothers in Guatemala were seen as ordinary criminal activity, not persecution.[43] The Tenth Circuit also

---

[37] Fatin v. INS, 12 F.3d 1233, 1243 (3d Cir. 1993) ("'[P]ersecution' is an extreme concept that does not include every sort of treatment our society regards as offensive."). *See also* Stanojkova v. Holder, 645 F.3d 943, 948 (7th Cir. 2011) ("The line between harassment and persecution is the line between the nasty and the barbaric, or alternatively between wishing you were living in another country and being so desperate that you flee without any assurance of being given refuge in any other country."); Mendez-Barrera v. Holder, 602 F.3d 21, 24 (1st Cir. 2010) ("In order to prove past persecution, an alien must show serious harm; a showing of persecution requires 'more than mere discomfiture, unpleasantness, harassment, or unfair treatment.'") (internal citations omitted).

[38] 536 F. App'x 243, 245 (3d Cir. 2013).

[39] *Id.*

[40] *Id.*

[41] *Id.* (citing *Jarbough v. Attorney General*, 483 F.3d 184, 187 (3d Cir. 2007) (upholding the denial of asylum to an alien who reported receiving bruises that did not require medical treatment while in the custody of Syrian officials on the grounds that the claim was time-barred) and *Li v. Attorney General*, 400 F.3d 157, 164 (3d Cir. 2005) ("[U]nfulfilled threats must be of a highly imminent and menacing nature in order to constitute persecution."). The stepbrother of the alien petitioner in *Martinez-Beltrand* was subsequently murdered in his home. However, the Third Circuit gave little weight to this because, while the alien suspected the gang was responsible for the murder, she had no knowledge of who killed her stepbrother, and the gang's last known encounter with her stepbrother was eight months before his demise. 536 F. App'x at 245.

[42] *Id.* (quoting *Abdille v. Ashcroft*, 242 F.3d 477, 494 (3d Cir. 2001) (denying petition for review as to the alien's request for asylum from South Africa because he had failed to prove persecution).

[43] 533 F. App'x 847, 848 (10th Cir. 2013).

emphasized that the alien petitioners were not "targeted" or singled out for harm on a protected ground,[44] a factor that some courts, in particular, note in their discussions of persecution.[45] However, the link between the harm suffered and any protected grounds is arguably better considered in conjunction with the "nexus" requirement in the *refugee* definition (see "On Account of"), and USCIS has explicitly instructed asylum officers to "separate the analysis of motivation from the evaluation of whether the harm is persecution, in order to make the basis of their decision as clear as possible."[46]

The harm suffered or feared must also have "some connection to governmental action or inaction."[47] In cases where the government is not directly responsible for the harm, this means showing that the government knowingly tolerates the harm inflicted by private parties, or is unwilling or unable to control the actions of these parties.[48] If such toleration, or unwillingness or inability to control, is found, the BIA and the federal courts may recognize harm arising to the level of persecution.[49] However, the BIA and the courts are sometimes reluctant to find an inability or unwillingness to control the actions of private persons based solely on the fact that the government's efforts have been ineffective. For example, in its 2005 decision in *Romero-Rodriguez v. U.S. Attorney General*, the U.S. Court of Appeals for the Eleventh Circuit upheld the denial of asylum to two brothers who fled alleged gang recruitment in Honduras.[50] In so doing, the court relied, in part, on the immigration judge's finding that the "Honduran government was attempting to control the lawlessness that exists in that country."[51] The U.S. Court of Appeals for the Seventh Circuit relied upon similar logic in its 2004 decision in *Lleshanaku v. Ashcroft*. There, the court upheld the denial of asylum to a woman who claimed to have been trailed and threatened by gang members in Albania on the grounds that she alleged "criminal racketeering [of a type] that almost all governments have trouble controlling, as opposed to the type of government conduct on which most grants of asylum are based."[52]

Both elements within the standard construction of *persecution*—i.e., the seriousness of the harm and government action or inaction—can be difficult to show in gang-related cases, as the foregoing examples illustrate. Indeed, as one court noted, the very pervasiveness of gang activity

---

[44] *Id.*

[45] *See, e.g.*, Kharkhan v. Ashcroft, 336 F.3d 601, 605 (7th Cir. 2003) (no persecution involved where removal to Ukraine would allegedly limit the alien's employment prospects and expose her to "the dangers of an uncontrolled criminal element" because the alien had not shown she would be "singled out" on a protected ground).

[46] U.S. Citizenship & Immigration Services, Refugee, Asylum and International Operations, Asylum Division, *Asylum Eligibility, Pt. I: Definition of Refugee, Definition of Persecution, Eligibility Based on Past Persecution*, Mar. 6, 2009, at 15-16 (copy on file with the author).

[47] *See, e.g.*, Orelien v. Gonzales, 467 F.3d 67, 72 (1st Cir. 2006) ("Persecution always implies some connection to governmental action or inaction.").

[48] *See, e.g.*, Kibinda v. Attorney General, 477 F.3d 113, 119 (3d Cir. 2007) ("forces the government is unable or unwilling to control"); Sangha v. INA, 103 F.3d 1482, 1487 (9th Cir. 1997) ("persons or organizations which the government is unable or unwilling to control").

[49] *See, e.g.*, Lopez-Soto v. Ashcroft, 383 F.3d 228, 234 (4th Cir. 2004) (noting, of the Mara 18 gang in Guatemala, that "there is no dispute that Petitioner has a well-founded fear of persecution by an organization which the government is unable to control"); *Ulloa Santos*, 552 F. App'x 199 n.1 (noting that the government of El Salvador had "publicly acknowledged" the failure of its "*mano duro*," or "firm hand," policy as to the gangs).

[50] 131 F. App'x. 203 (11th Cir. 2005).

[51] *Id.* at 204.

[52] 100 F. App'x. 546, 549 (7th Cir. 2004). *See also In re* McMullan, 17 I. & N. Dec. 542, 544 (BIA 1980) ("We do not agree that the respondent has established that the government in Ireland will be unable or unwilling to protect the respondent from the [Provisional Irish Republican Army].").

---

within a society can make a finding of persecution less likely,[53] insofar as gang actions can be characterized as "widespread violence" or "ordinary criminal activity."[54]

"Well-Founded Fear"

A showing of past persecution gives rise to a rebuttable presumption that the alien has a well-founded fear of future persecution.[55] Otherwise, absent a showing of past persecution, the alien must show that he or she has a "well-founded fear" of future persecution in order to be eligible for asylum in the United States.[56] Federal regulations further provide that applicants for asylum have a well-founded fear of persecution if

> (A) [t]he applicant has a fear of persecution in his or her country of nationality or, if stateless, in his or her country of last habitual residence, on account of race, religion, nationality, membership in a particular social group, or political opinion; (B) [t]here is a reasonable possibility of suffering such persecution if he or she were to return to that country; and (C) [h]e or she is unable or unwilling to return to, or avail himself or herself of the protection of, that country because of such fear.[57]

As these regulations suggest, the test for whether aliens have a well-founded fear of persecution is partly subjective in that it focuses upon whether the alien actually "has a fear of persecution."[58] The subjective element is satisfied if the applicant's fear of persecution is genuine.[59] A genuine

---

[53] *See Orellana-Monson*, 685 F.3d at 522 ("The sad part about [the alien's asylum] claim is that it ultimately fails because of the pervasive nature of Mara 18 against any non-gang member in El Salvadoran society.").

[54] *Mendez-Barrera*, 602 F.3d at 25 (widespread violence, affecting all citizens, does not establish persecution on a protected ground); Boci v. Gonzales, 473 F.3d 762, 767 (7th Cir. 2007) ("widespread lawlessness"); *Abdille*, 242 F.3d at 494 ("[O]rdinary criminal activity does not rise to the level of persecution necessary to establish eligibility for asylum."); *Ulloa Santos*, 552 F. App'x. at 201 ("[A]cts by criminals are not persecution.") (internal quotations omitted); Perez-Perez v. Holder, 500 F. App'x. 684 (9th Cir. 2012) (MS 13 gang "bothers everybody," not just or primarily Christians).

[55] 8 C.F.R. §208.13(b)(1). This presumption may be rebutted if (1) there has been a "fundamental change" in circumstances such that the applicant no longer has a well-founded fear of persecution on account of a protected ground; or (2) the applicant could avoid future persecution by relocating to another part of the country. *See* 8 C.F.R. §208.13(b)(1)(i)(A)-(B). A showing of past persecution could also, in especially severe cases, potentially permit the alien to remain in the United States even if he or she does not have a well-founded fear of future persecution. *See* 8 C.F.R. §208.13(b)(1)(iii)(A)-(B) (permitting the grant of asylum in the absence of a well-founded fear of persecution where (1) the applicant demonstrates "compelling reasons" for being unwilling or unable to return to his or her home country on account of the "severity" of the past persecution, or (2) the applicant establishes there is a "reasonable possibility" he or she would suffer "other serious harm" if removed to that country).

[56] *See* 8 C.F.R. §208.13(b) ("The applicant may qualify as a refugee either because he or she has suffered past persecution or because he or she has a well-founded fear of future persecution.").

[57] 8 C.F.R. §208.13(b)(2)(A)-(C).

[58] *See, e.g.*, Guevara-Flores v. INS, 786 F.2d 1242, 1249 (5th Cir. 1986) ("[T]he well-founded fear of persecution standard is at least partially subjective, because fear is a state of apprehension or anxiety not usually subject to rational measurement. The standard is only partially subjective, however, because it requires that the fear be a well-founded one. The alien's fear must have some basis in the reality of the circumstances; mere irrational apprehension is insufficient to meet the alien's burden of proof.") (internal citations omitted); *Martinez-Beltrand*, 536 F. App'x at 246 ("A future-persecution claim requires the applicant to demonstrate a subjective fear of persecution and that her fear is objectively reasonable.") (internal quotations and citations omitted).

[59] *See, e.g., In re Acosta*, 19 I. & N. Dec. 211, 221 (BIA 1985) (equating fear with a "a genuine apprehension or awareness of danger"), *overruled on other grounds by Matter of* Mogharrabi, 19 I. & N. Dec. 439 (BIA 1987).

---

fear of persecution must be the applicant's "primary motive" in seeking asylum, but it need not be the only motive.[60]

On the other hand, the test for a well-founded fear of persecution is also objective in that there must be a "reasonable possibility" that the alien would suffer persecution if returned to his or her home country.[61] The regulations do not define what is meant by a *reasonable possibility* of persecution. However, the Supreme Court helped establish the meaning of this term with its 1987 decision in *INS v. Cardoza-Fonseca*, which found that "[o]ne can ... have a well-founded fear of an event happening when there is less than a 50% chance of the occurrence taking place."[62] Following the *Cardoza-Fonseca* decision, the BIA emphasized that determinations as to whether a fear is well-founded ultimately rest not on the statistical probability of persecution occurring, but on whether a reasonable person in the alien's position would fear persecution.[63] Federal courts have generally deferred to the BIA on the meaning of *reasonable possibility*, with some courts opining that a reasonable possibility of persecution can exist where there is as little as a one-in-ten chance of the feared harm occurring.[64]

A well-founded fear of persecution has been found to be lacking in some gang-related asylum cases, often in cases where past harms are not viewed as persecution.[65] The genuineness of the alien's fear is often not in doubt.[66] However, such fear can be seen as unreasonable in light of the circumstances.[67]

---

[60] *See* U.S. Citizenship & Immigration Services, Refugee, Asylum and International Operations, Asylum Division, *Asylum Eligibility, Pt. II: Well-Founded Fear*, Mar. 6, 2009, at 4 (copy on file with the author).

[61] *See supra* note 58.

[62] *Cardoza-Fonseca*, 480 U.S. at 431 ("One can certainly have a well-founded fear of an event happening when there is less than a 50% chance of the occurrence taking place. As one leading authority has pointed out: "Let us ... presume that it is known that in the applicant's country of origin every tenth adult male person is either put to death or sent to some remote labor camp.... In such a case it would be only too apparent that anyone who has managed to escape from the country in question will have [a] 'well-founded fear of being persecuted' upon his eventual return.")

[63] *See, e.g., Matter of* Mogharrabi, 19 I. & N. Dec. 439 (BIA 1987). In this decision, the BIA also restated four specific "elements" that aliens must show in order to demonstrate a well-founded fear of persecution. *Id.* at 446. In their current articulation, these elements include (1) the alien possesses, or is believed to possess, a characteristic that the persecutor seeks to overcome; (2) the persecutor is aware or could become aware that the alien possesses (or is believed to possess) the characteristic; (3) the persecutor has the capability to persecute the applicant; and (4) the persecutor has the inclination to persecute the applicant. *See Asylum Eligibility, Pt. II*, *supra* note 60, at 6-7.

[64] *See* Arteaga v. INS, 836 F.2d 1227, 1232-1233 (9th Cir. 1988) ("The Supreme Court has suggested that a one-in-ten chance of the feared event occurring would make the fear well-founded.").

[65] *See, e.g., Martinez-Beltrand*, 536 F. App'x at 245; *Cosenza-Cruz*, 533 F. App'x. at 848.

[66] *See, e.g., Kibinda*, 477 F.3d at 118 (court relying on the immigration judge's finding that the alien had a "genuine subjective fear of persecution").

[67] *See, e.g., id.* at 119-120 (court finding that the alien's fear, while genuinely held, was objectively unreasonable since there was "ample evidence" in the record that the alien had "always been valued and trusted" by the government entity from which he feared persecution).

What Role Does a "Credible Fear of Persecution" Play in the Asylum Process?

Having a "credible fear of persecution" is not a requirement for asylum under Section 208 of the INA. Instead, a credible fear of persecution is only required with (1) aliens subject to expedited removal under Section 235(b) of the INA (typically arriving aliens who have no documents or fraudulent documents) and (2) UACs from Canada and Mexico. Aliens subject to expedited removal can generally be ordered removed by immigration officers without formal removal proceedings before an immigration judge. However, there is an exception for aliens who indicate either an intention to apply for asylum or a "fear of persecution." These aliens are referred to USCIS asylum officers for further interviews and, if determined to have a credible fear of persecution, are detained for consideration of their asylum applications. (Those whom the asylum officer finds do not have a credible fear of persecution can obtain review of this determination by an immigration judge.)

Analogous procedures apply with UACs from "contiguous countries" (i.e., Canada and Mexico). Section 235 of the William Wilberforce Trafficking Victims Protection Reauthorization Act (TVPRA) of 2008 (P.L. 110-457) requires that UACs from these countries be screened to determine whether they have a credible fear of persecution if returned to their home country. Those who are determined not to have such a fear—and who meet certain other criteria (e.g., are not victims of a "severe form of trafficking in persons")—may be permitted to withdraw their applications for admission and be returned to their home countries. However, those who are found to have a credible fear of persecution (or who do not meet the other criteria or consent to voluntary return) are placed in formal removal proceedings, just like UACs from noncontiguous countries.

Congress defined *credible fear of persecution* for purposes of expedited removal to mean that "there is a significant possibility, taking into account the credibility of statements made by the alien in support of the alien's claim and such other facts as are known to the officer, that the alien could establish eligibility for asylum." However, the meaning of the term *significant possibility* is not defined by statute or regulation. Instead, it has been informally construed by the executive branch to mean a "substantial and realistic possibility of succeeding" in asylum proceedings. This interpretation is apparently based on case law construing similar language in other contexts, as well as legislative history materials describing the credible-fear standard as a "low screening standard for admission into the usual full asylum process."

In contrast, Congress did not define credible fear of persecution for purposes of the TVPRA, nor has the executive branch done so by regulation. However, the canon of statutory interpretation holding that the same term used in related statutes is generally read the same way each time it appears, would seem to support the view that credible fear is to be construed in the same way for purposes of the TVPRA as it is for the INA.

See generally INA §235(b), 8 U.S.C. §1225(b); 8 U.S.C. §1232; U.S. Citizenship and Immigration Services, *Asylum Officer Basic Training: Credible Fear*, Apr. 14, 2006 (copy on file with the author).

"On Account of"

The *refugee* definition's proviso that the persecution be "on account of" a protected ground has been construed to require that there be a "nexus" between the harm that the alien has incurred or fears and the alien's race, religion, nationality, political opinion, or membership in a particular social group. To establish the requisite nexus, the alien must provide some evidence (direct or circumstantial) that the persecutor is motivated to persecute the victim because the victim possesses—or is believed to possess—the protected characteristic.[68] The alien need not prove the actual, exact reason for the persecution. Rather, he or she need only establish facts on which a reasonable person would fear that the danger "arises on account of ... race, religion, nationality, membership in a particular social group, or political opinion."[69] However, as a result of amendments made to Section 208 of the INA by the REAL ID Act of 2005 (P.L. 109-13), the

---

[68] INS v. Elias-Zacarias, 502 U.S. 478, 483 (1992) ("[The alien petitioner] objects that he cannot be expected to provide direct proof of his persecutors' motives. We do not require that. But since the statute makes motive critical, he must provide some evidence of it, direct or circumstantial.").

[69] *Matter of* Fuentes, 19 I. &N. Dec. 658, 662 (BIA 1988).

---

alien must also show his or her race, religion, nationality, political opinion, or membership in a particular social group "was or will be at least one central reason" for his or her persecution.[70] A *central reason* has been construed to mean a reason that is more than "incidental, tangential, superficial, or subordinate to another reason for harm."[71] A central reason need not be the only reason, or even a "primary" reason, though. So-called "mixed motive" claims—where the persecutor is motivated by the alien's possession of a protected characteristic as well as other factors (e.g., greed, revenge)—are still possible post-REAL ID Act.[72]

Lack of the requisite nexus between the alleged persecution and a protected ground is another reason that gang-related asylum claims may fail. For example, in its 2011 decision in *Bueso-Avila v. Holder*, the Seventh Circuit upheld the executive branch's denial of asylum to an alien who claimed to have been persecuted by gangs in Honduras because of his Evangelical Christian religion.[73] The Seventh Circuit did so, in part, because it viewed the executive branch's conclusion that the gang was either unaware of or unconcerned about the alien's religious beliefs as "legitimate" in light of "all the evidence" presented by the alien.[74] The U.S. Court of Appeals for the First Circuit relied upon similar logic in its 2012 decision in *Carreanza-Vargas v. Holder*. There, in upholding the executive branch's denial of asylum to alien who claimed to fear persecution by gangs in El Salvador based on his membership in the particular social group of "former police and army members who fear harm by gangs," the First Circuit noted that the evidence supported the conclusion that the gangs were motivated by economic gain, not the alien's membership in any particular social group.[75] As these examples suggest, conventional understandings of gangs' motives can shape the outcomes in these cases, with courts upholding denials of asylum where the evidence can be seen as demonstrating "typical" gang activities (e.g., robbery, extortion, recruitment of new members).[76]

Protected Grounds

The *refugee* definition encompasses five so-called protected grounds: race, religion, nationality, political opinion, and membership in a particular social group. Gang-related asylum claims have

---

[70] INA §208(b)(1)(B)(i).

[71] Quinteros-Mendoza v. Holder, 556 F.3d 159, 164 (4th Cir. 2009) (quoting *In re J-B-N-*, 24 I. & N. Dec. 208, 214 (BIA 2007) (dismissing the alien's appeal of the denial of his application for asylum where the "fact that the [aliens] were born in Burundi and then came to live in Rwanda can best be described as incidental to the central land dispute").

[72] *See, e.g., J-B-N- & S-M-*, 24 I. & N. Dec. at 212 ("The definition of the word 'central' includes '[h]aving dominant power, influence, or control.' Recognizing that this definition could pose problems for those seeking asylum based on 'mixed motives,' Congress purposely did not require that the protected ground be the central reason for the actions of the persecutors. Rather, the version of the REAL ID Act originally introduced in the House of Representatives provided that an asylum applicant would bear the burden of proving that one of the five protected grounds 'was or will be a central reason for persecuting the applicant.' During conference on the bill, this language was modified to become 'at least one central reason.... That language thus confirms that aliens whose persecutors were motivated by more than one reason continue to be protected ... if they can show a nexus to a protected ground.") (internal citations omitted).

[73] 663 F.3d 934 (7th Cir. 2011), *en banc reh'g denied*, 2012 U.S. App. LEXIS 4780 (7th Cir., Mar. 1, 2012).

[74] 663 F.3d at 938.

[75] 492 F. App'x 133, 136 (1st Cir. 2012).

[76] It should also be noted that the courts have generally upheld denials of asylum based on lack of a nexus even where the executive branch has not addressed whether a protected ground, in fact, exists. *See, e.g.*, Hernandez Tumacaj, 535 F. App'x 873, 875 (11th Cir. 2013). Such decisions can be taken to mean that the evidence presented by the alien in support of his or her claim for asylum is such that it could be construed to demonstrate only gangs acting as gangs do, nothing more, regardless of whether any protected ground exists.

---

been made on various grounds, including religion and political opinion.[77] The most common ground, however, has arguably been membership in a particular social group, a construct which has been described as "an especially contested and problematic area in asylum law."[78] Particular social group is the ground upon which all asylum claims not based on race, religion, nationality, or political opinion must be made. However, the executive branch and the federal courts have been reluctant to treat "particular social group" as a "catch-all," permitting anyone who experiences harm anywhere in the world to obtain refugee status or asylum in the United States.[79] This reluctance would appear to underlie, in part, the evolution in the executive branch's construction of the term *particular social group* between 1985 and the present, a development which some commentators have suggested underlies the failure of many gang-based asylum claims.[80]

Evolution in the Construction of *Particular Social Group*

Because there is no statutory or regulatory definition of *particular social group*, the BIA has established the meaning of this term through case-by-case adjudication, beginning with its 1985 decision in *Matter of Acosta*. The alien in *Acosta* claimed to fear persecution in El Salvador because he co-founded and actively participated in a cooperative organization of taxi drivers—known as COTAXI—that refused to participate in work stoppages allegedly requested by anti-government guerillas.[81] However, the immigration judge denied the alien asylum because he found the alien's testimony insufficient to prove the alleged harm.[82] The BIA affirmed this denial on other grounds, including on the grounds that the particular social group proposed by the alien—"COTAXI drivers and persons engaged in the transportation industry of El Salvador"—was not cognizable under the INA.[83] The BIA reached this conclusion by resorting to the doctrine

---

[77] *See, e.g.*, *Bueso-Avila v. Holder*, 663 F.3d 934 (7th Cir. 2011), *en banc reh'g denied*, 2012 U.S. App. LEXIS 4780 (7th Cir., Mar. 1, 2012) (religion); Cosenza-Cruz v. Holder, 533 F. App'x 847 (10th Cir. 2013) (political opinion); Castillo Sanchez v. U.S. Attorney General, 523 F. App'x 682 (11th Cir. 2013) (same).

[78] *Gang-Related Asylum Claims*, *supra* note 10, at 829.

[79] *See, e.g.*, Castillo-Arias v. U.S. Attorney General, 446 F.3d 1190, 1198 (11th Cir. 2006) ("'[P]articular social group' should not be a 'catch all' for all persons alleging persecution who do not fit elsewhere."); Solis-Gonzalez v. Holder, 523 F. App'x 320, 321 (6th Cir. 2013) ("This 'narrowing' requirement enforces the recognition that 'the social group category was not meant to be a "catch all" applicable to all persons fearing persecution.'"); *In re H-*, 21 I. & N. Dec. 337, 350 (BIA 1996) (Heilman, J., dissenting) (majority's recognition of a particular social group comprised of clan members who were targeted in a civil war a "quixotic attempt to right the wrongs of the world through the asylum process").

[80] *See, e.g.*, *Challenging the "Political," supra* note 3, at 244 (characterizing grants of asylum based on gang persecution as "rare"); *Gang-Related Asylum Claims*, *supra* note 10, at 828 (persons with gang cases having "serious difficulties in successfully applying for asylum"); Lindsay M. Harris & Morgan M. Weibel, *Matter of S-E-G-: The Final Nail in the Coffin for Gang-Related Asylum Claims?*, 20 BERKELEY LA RAZA L.J. 5, 23 (2010) ("With the exception of the Seventh Circuit's grant of withholding in *Benitez Ramos*, Circuit courts have uniformly denied gang-related claims."). *See also* Mayorga-Vidal v. Holder, 675 F.3d 9, 14 (1st Cir. 2012) ("Because discrete groups meeting the immutable characteristic requisite—such as racial or ethnic groups ...—are already independently afforded protected status, successful 'stand-alone social group claims are rather rare.'"); Ramirez-Canenguez v. Holder, 528 F. App'x 853, 854 (10th Cir. 2013) ("Harassment by gangs rarely arises from a protected attribute such as political opinion or membership in a particular social group.").

[81] 19 I. & N. Dec. at 216-217. The alien fled to the United States after his organization and other similar organizations received a number of anonymous threats. Taxis were also seized and burned, and five COTAXI founders and officers were killed after receiving anonymous notes threatening their lives. *Id.*

[82] *Id.* at 218.

[83] *Id.* at 232, 234.

---

of *eiusdem generis* in construing the meaning of the words "particular social group."[84] In keeping with the doctrine's holding that "general words used in an enumeration with specific words should be construed in a manner consistent with the specific words," the BIA considered "particular social group" in conjunction with "race," "religion," "nationality," and "political opinion," and noted that each of the other grounds "describes persecution aimed at an immutable characteristic: a characteristic that either is beyond the power of an individual to change or is so fundamental to individual identity or conscience that it ought not be required to be changed." Thus, it concluded, "particular social group" is to be construed as describing a "group of persons all of whom share a common, immutable characteristic." According to the BIA, this characteristic can be "innate," such as "sex, color, or kinship ties," or based on "shared past experiences," such as former military leadership or land ownership. However, it cannot be based on something that is "not immutable," and the BIA viewed driving a taxi or refusing to participate in work stoppages as not immutable.[85]

The federal courts generally deferred to the BIA's construction of *particular social group* in *Acosta*, finding that it constituted a "reasonable" and "permissible" interpretation of an ambiguous statutory term.[86] Similarly, the UNHCR incorporated *Acosta*'s construction of this term into its own definition of *particular social group*,[87] suggesting that it viewed the BIA's interpretation as consistent with the Convention and Protocol.

Despite this deference, the BIA revisited and reformulated the meaning of particular social group in its 2006 decision in *Matter of C-A-*. There, the BIA rejected aliens' challenge to the denial of

---

[84] *Id.* at 233.

[85] *Id.* Here, the BIA noted that the members of COTAXI could avoid the threats of the guerrillas either by changing jobs or by cooperating in the work stoppages. It also noted that "the internationally accepted concept of a refugee simply does not guarantee an individual a right to work in the job of his choice." *Id.* Others have disputed the latter premise, suggesting that the right to a "free choice of employment" is a fundamental right, the deprivation of which could constitute persecution. *See, e.g.*, Universal Declaration of Human Rights, at Art. 23(1).

[86] *See, e.g.*, Alvarez-Flores v. INS, 909 F.2d 1, 7 (1st Cir. 1990); Fatin v. INS, 12 F.3d 1233, 1239-1240 (3d Cir. 1993); Ontunez-Tursios v. Ashcroft, 303 F.3d 341, 362 (5th Cir. 2002); Castellano-Chacon v. INS, 341 F.3d 533, 546-548 (6th Cir. 2003); Lwin v. INS, 144 F.3d 505, 512 (7th Cir. 1998); Safaie v. INS, 25 F.3d 636, 640 (8th Cir. 1994); Niang v. Gonzales, 422 F.3d 1187, 1198 (10th Cir. 2005); Velasquez-Otero v. U.S. Attorney General, 456 F. App'x 822, 825 (11th Cir. 2012) ("Because Congress did not define 'particular social group,' we defer to the BIA's formulation from *Matter of Acosta*."). Initially, the Ninth Circuit departed from the *Acosta* formulation by requiring a "voluntary associational relationship" among group members. *See* Sanchez-Trujillo v. INS, 801 F.2d 1571, 1576 (9th Cir. 1986) ("[The] phrase 'particular social group' implies a collection of people closely affiliated with each other, who are actuated by some common impulse or interest. Of central concern is the existence of a voluntary associational relationship among the purported members, which imparts some common characteristic that is fundamental to their identity as a member of that discrete social group."). However, following criticism by the Seventh Circuit in *Lwin*, the Ninth Circuit subsequently merged its "voluntary association" requirement with the "common, immutable characteristic" requirement of *Acosta* in its 2000 decision in *Hernandez-Montiel v. INS. See* 225 F.3d 1084, 1087 (9th Cir. 2000), *overruled on other grounds*, Thomas v. Gonzales, 409 F.3d 1177 (9th Cir. 2005). Some other circuits that generally deferred to *Acosta* also required, or considered as an element, the social perception of the group, a development which arguably presaged the BIA's decision in *Matter of C-A-*, discussed below. *See, e.g.*, Gomez v. INS, 947 F.2d 660, 664 (2d Cir. 1991) ("A particular social group is comprised of individuals who possess some fundamental characteristic in common which serves to distinguish them in the eyes of a persecutor—or in the eyes of the outside world in general.").

[87] *See* UNHCR, Guidelines on International Protection: "Membership of a Particular Social Group" within the Context of Article 1A(2) of the 1951 Convention and/or its 1967 Protocol Relating to the Status of Refugees, May 7, 2002, at 3, *available at* http://www.unhcr.org/3d58de2da html ("A particular social group is a group of persons who share a common characteristic other than their risk of being persecuted, or who are perceived as a group by society. The characteristic will often be one which is innate, unchangeable, or which is otherwise fundamental to identity, conscience or the exercise of one's human rights.").

---

their asylum application after finding that "noncriminal informants"—specifically, informants against the Cali drug cartel in Columbia—do not constitute a particular social group for purposes of the INA.[88] In so finding, the BIA retained *Acosta*'s requirement that members of a particular social group share a common, immutable characteristic, but emphasized the further requirement that the group be "recognizable" as such (i.e., possess "social visibility").[89] The BIA did so, in part, because it viewed the specific social groups based on innate characteristics, recognized pursuant to previous applications of the standard articulated in *Acosta*, as "generally easily recognizable and understood by others to constitute social groups."[90] In contrast, it viewed the proposed social group of noncriminal informants as different because

> the very nature of the conduct at issue is such that it is generally out of the public view. In the normal course of events, an informant against the Cali cartel intends to remain unknown and undiscovered. Recognizability or visibility is limited to those informants who are discovered because they appear as witnesses or otherwise come to the attention of cartel members.[91]

The BIA also noted that the proposed grouping of noncriminal informants was "too loosely defined to meet the requirement of particularity," since it could include persons who "passed along information concerning any of the numerous guerrilla factions or narco-trafficking cartels currently active in Colombia to the Government or to a competing faction or cartel."[92]

Two years later, in its 2008 decision in *Matter of S-E-G-*, the BIA applied the social visibility and particularity requirements to three siblings who had fled alleged persecution by the MS-13 gang in El Salvador. There, in affirming the immigration judge's denial of asylum, the BIA found that the siblings' proposed group of "Salvadoran youth who have been subjected to recruitment efforts by MS-13 and who have rejected or resisted membership based on their own personal, moral, and religious opposition to the gang's values and activities" lacked both social visibility and particularity.[93] As to social visibility, the BIA emphasized that the purported group was not recognized as a discrete class of persons by Salvadoran society.[94] Similarly, as to particularity, the BIA noted that the group lacked well-defined boundaries, such that it could be readily determined who fell within, or outside of, the group.[95] Further, the BIA noted that the youths' attempt to limit their proposed group by claiming it was comprised of male children who "lack stable families and meaningful adult protection" and "who are from middle and low income classes" relied upon "amorphous" characteristics, as "people's ideas of what those terms mean can vary."[96]

---

[88] 23 I. & N. Dec. 951, 957-961 (BIA 2006).

[89] *Id.* at 959-961.

[90] *Id.* at 959-960 (noting that "Filipinos of mixed Filipino-Chinese ancestry;" "young women of the Tchamba-Junsuntu tribe of northern Togo who did not undergo female genital mutilation as practiced by that tribe and who opposed the practice;" "members of the Marehan subclan of Somalia who share ties of kinship and linguistic commonalities;" "persons identified as homosexuals by the Cuban government;" and "former members of the national police of El Salvador" had all been viewed as cognizable social groups under the precedent of *Acosta*).

[91] *Id.* at 960.

[92] *Id.* at 957.

[93] 24 I. & N. Dec. 579, 582-583 (BIA 2008). The BIA also rejected a related proposed group comprised of the family members of such youth. *Id.*

[94] *Id.* at 586. The BIA further noted that the youth allegedly recruited by gangs are "not in a substantially different situation from anyone who has crossed the gang, or who is perceived to be a threat to the gang's interests." *Id.* at 587.

[95] *Id.* at 585.

[96] *Id.* The BIA further suggested that it viewed the requisite "nexus" between a protected ground and any persecution as (continued...)

The BIA's decisions in *Matter of C-A-* and *Matter of S-E-G-* prompted a somewhat different response than its earlier decision in *Matter of Acosta*. While most federal courts of appeals deferred to the BIA's revised interpretation of *particular social group*,[97] two did not. First, the Seventh Circuit rejected the "social visibility" requirement in its 2009 decision in *Gatimi v. Holder*, in part, on the grounds that it was inconsistent with the BIA's prior decisions, and the BIA did not articulate a principled reason for the change.[98] The Seventh Circuit also indicated that it viewed the BIA's discussion of social visibility as referring to literal or ocular visibility,[99] an interpretation that has elsewhere been suggested to constitute an impermissible construction of the INA.[100] Subsequently, the Third Circuit relied on similar reasoning as to social visibility—and also rejected the particularity requirement—in its 2011 decision in *Valdiviezo-Galdamez v. Attorney General*. The Third Circuit did so, in part, because it viewed particularity as "little more than a reworked definition" of the "discredited requirement of 'social visability.'"[101] The UNHCR also objected to the BIA's construction of particular social group in *Matter of C-A-* and its application to gang-related asylum claims in *Matter of S-E-G-*. Among other things, the UNHCR filed an amicus brief with the BIA in *Matter of Thomas* in 2007, calling for the BIA to eliminate the "social visibility" and "particularity" requirements and return to the "common, immutable characteristic" standard of *Acosta*.[102] The UNHCR also petitioned Attorney General Holder in 2009 to certify *Matter of S-E-G-* to himself for review.[103] In both cases, the UNHCR asserted that the executive branch's construction of *particular social group* was inconsistent with UNHCR guidance and U.S. obligations under international law.

Subsequently, the BIA revisited and reformulated the construction of *particular social group* once more in its 2014 decisions in *Matter of W-G-R-* and *Matter of M-E-V-G-*.[104] In these two decisions, issued on the same day, the BIA retained the requirements that particular social groups possess common, immutable characteristics and particularity, but renamed the former "social

---

(...continued)

lacking, since "there is no evidence in the record to show that gang members limit recruitment efforts to male children who fit the above description, or do so in order to punish them for these characteristics, although these factors perhaps make the potential recruit an easier and more desirable target." *Id.*

[97] *See, e.g.*, Scatambuli v. Holder, 558 F.3d 53 (1st Cir. 2009); Jiang v. Mukasey, 296 F. App'x 166, 168 (2d Cir. 2008); Flores v. Mukasey, 297 F. App'x 389 (6th Cir. 2008); Davila-Mejia v. Mukasey, 531 F.3d 624 (8th Cir. 2008); Santos-Lemus v. Mukasey, 542 F.3d 738 (9th Cir. 2008), *abrogated on other grounds* by Ramos-Lopez v. Holder, 563 F.3d 855 (9th Cir. 2009); Gomez-Benitez v. U.S. Attorney General, 295 F. App'x 324 (11th Cir. 2008).

[98] 578 F.3d 611, 616 (7th Cir. 2009) ("[T]he Board has been inconsistent. ... When an administrative agency's decisions are inconsistent, a court cannot pick one of the inconsistent lines and defer to that one, unless only one is within the scope of the agency's discretion to interpret the statutes it enforces or to make policy.").

[99] *Id.* at 615.

[100] *See, e.g.*, Henriquez-Rivas v. Holder, 707 F.3d 1081, 1087-1088 (9th Cir. 2013) ("We agree that a requirement of 'on-sight' visibility would be inconsistent with previous BIA decisions and likely impermissible under the statute."); *Rivera-Barrientos*, 666 F.3d at 652 ("If we agreed with the Seventh Circuit's understanding of the social visibility test [as requiring ocular visibility], we might also find it problematic.").

[101] 663 F.3d at 608.

[102] In Matter of Thomas, No. A75-597-033/-034/-035/-036, Brief of the Office of the UNHCR as Amicus Curiae, Jan. 25, 2007, *available at* http://www refworld.org/docid/45c34c244 html.

[103] UNHCR, Matter of S-E-G-, 24 I. & N. Dec. 579 (BIA 2008), Mar. 18, 2009, *available at* http://www.ilcm.org/litigation/AG_certification_amicus_UNHCR.pdf.

[104] *Matter of* W-G-R-, 26 I. & N. Dec. 208 (BIA 2014); *Matter of* M-E-V-G-, 26 I. & N. Dec. 227 (BIA 2014).

---

visibility" requirement as "social distinction."[105] In so doing, the BIA emphasized that it viewed social distinction as

> referr[ing] to recognition by society, taking as its basis the plain language of the Act—in this case, the word 'social.' To be socially distinct, a group need not be *seen* by society; it must instead be *perceived* as a group by society. Members of the group may be visibly recognizable, but society can also consider persons to be a group without being able to identify the members by sight.[106]

Particular Social Group: How Does the UNHCR's Construction Compare to Domestic Law?

One of the ways in which the UNHCR's construction of the *refugee* definition differs from that of U.S. law involves the meaning of *particular social group*. The UNHCR definition of this term encompasses individuals who either (1) share a common characteristic other than their risk of being persecuted, *or* (2) are perceived as a group by society. In other words, groups that share a common characteristic, but are not perceived as a group by society, would qualify. The same is true of groups that do not share a common characteristic, but are perceived as a group by society.

The BIA, in contrast, has required that a group *both* share a common immutable characteristic *and* be perceived as such by society (i.e., possess social distinction and particularity). Under the BIA's interpretation, a group that shares a common immutable characteristic, but is not perceived as such by society, cannot constitute a particular social group.

See generally UNHCR, Guidelines on International Protection: "Membership of a Particular Social Group" within the Context of Article 1A(2) of the 1951 Convention and/or its 1967 Protocol Relating to the Status of Refugees, May 7, 2002; *Matter of W-G-R-*, 26 I. & N. Dec. 208 (BIA 2014); *Matter of M-E-V-G-*, 26 I. & N. Dec. 227 (BIA 2014).

The BIA also emphasized that it viewed the requirement of social distinction as consistent with prior BIA precedents recognizing "young tribal women who are opposed to female genital mutilation," "homosexuals in Cuba," and "former national police members," among others, as particular social groups.[107] Further, while acknowledging that its approach differs from UNHCR guidelines, the BIA noted that its approach is similar to that adopted by the European Union, which "also declines to follow the ... definition set forth by the UNHCR."[108]

It remains to be seen whether federal courts of appeals will defer to the BIA's "social visibility" requirement in determining what constitutes a particular social group for purposes of refugee status and asylum.[109] However, the evolution in the construction of the term *particular social group* arguably helps explain the limited success of gang-related asylum claims to date.[110] Especially since the BIA's decision in *Matter of C-A-*, these claims have generally failed, in part, because the various social groups articulated by individual aliens are seen as lacking social visibility and/or particularity. Some commentators have suggested that the BIA's recent shift from "social visibility" to "social distinction" could potentially make it more

---

[105] *See* 26 I. & N. Dec. at 216 ("Our definition of 'social visibility' clarified the importance of 'perception' or 'recognition' in the concept of the particular social group. The term was never meant to be read literally."); 26 I. & N. Dec. at 237 (similar).

[106] 26 I. & N. Dec. at 216.

[107] *Id.* at 217.

[108] *Id.* at 220.

[109] *See, e.g.*, Pirir-Boc v. Holder, No. 09-73671, 2014 U.S. App. LEXIS 8577, at *22 (9th Cir., May 7, 2014) (noting that the meaning of the term particular social group is "in flux, and it is premature to determine precisely how the rule [articulated in the BIA's recent decisions] will be implemented").

[110] *See supra* note 80.

---

difficult for aliens to obtain asylum by requiring that aliens produce sociological studies or other evidence demonstrating that the alien's home society recognizes the group as distinct.[111] On the other hand, given the deference that the courts have generally afforded to the executive branch's construction of *particular social group*, this term and/or *social distinction* could conceivably be reinterpreted by the executive branch in the future to make it easier for aliens to obtain asylum on account of membership in a particular social group.

Specific Social Groups

While the particular social groups proposed in individual cases vary somewhat in their specific formulations, they can generally be seen as involving one of four broad categories: (1) persons resistant to gang recruitment; (2) former gang members; (3) witnesses and informants against gangs; and (4) the family members of persons in the foregoing groups. Most courts have not considered these proposed groupings as constituting particular social groups for purposes of granting asylum, although groups involving former gang members, witnesses or informants against the gangs, and family members may be cognizable as particular social groups in certain jurisdictions.

Persons Resistant to Gang Recruitment

In a number of cases, courts have upheld the denial of asylum to aliens based on their purported membership in particular social groups made up of persons who are targeted for or resist gang recruitment, generally because the courts view the proposed group as lacking both social visibility (now, distinction) and/or particularity.[112] For example, in its 2012 decision in *Mayorga-Vidal v.*

---

[111] *See, e.g.*, Ashley Huebner & Lisa Koop, New BIA Decisions Undermine U.S. Obligations to Protect Asylum Seekers, Nat'l Immigrant Justice Center, Feb. 18, 2014, *available at* http://www.immigrantjustice.org/litigation/blog/new-bia-decisions-undermine-us-obligations-protect-asylum-seekers.

[112] *See, e.g.*, Umaña-Ramos v. Holder, 724 F.3d 667 (8th Cir. 2013) ("young Salvadorans who have refused recruitment by the Mara Salvatrucha gang" not a cognizable social group for purposes of asylum); Lopez-Mendez v. Holder, 698 F.3d 675 (8th Cir. 2012) ("persons resistant to gang recruitment" not cognizable); Beltrand-Alas v. Holder, 689 F.3d 90 (1st Cir. 2012) ("persons who oppose gangs" not cognizable); Orellana-Monson v. Holder, 685 F.3d 511 (5th Cir. 2011) ("males, ages 8 to 15, who have been recruited by Mara 18 but have refused to join due to a principled opposition to gangs" not cognizable); Garcia Callejas v. Holder, 666 F.3d 828 (1st Cir. 2012) (young males targeted for recruitment not cognizable); Rivera-Barrientos v. Holder, 666 F.3d 641 (10th Cir. 2012) ("El Salvadoran women between the ages of 12 and 25 who have resisted gang recruitment" not cognizable); Constanza v. Holder, 647 F.3d 749 (8th Cir. 2011) ("persons resistant to gang membership" and "persons who fear harm to their families from gangs" not cognizable); Larious v. Holder, 608 F.3d 105 (1st Cir. 2010) ("young Guatemalan men recruited by gang members who resist such recruitment" and "street children" not cognizable); Mendez-Barrera v. Holder, 602 F.3d 21 (1st Cir. 2010) ("young women recruited by gang members who resist such recruitment" not cognizable); Ramos-Lopez v. Holder, 563 F.3d 855 (9th Cir. 2009) ("young Honduran men who have been recruited by the MS-13, but who refuse to join" not cognizable), *abrogated, in part, on other grounds by* Iraheta v. Holder, 532 F. App'x 703 (9th Cir. 2013); Santos-Lemus v. Mukasey, 542 F.3d 738 (9th Cir. 2008), *abrogated, in part, on other grounds by* Ramos-Lopez v. Holder, 563 F.3d 855 (9th Cir. 2009) ("class of young men in El Salvador who resist the violence and intimidation of gang rule" not cognizable); Escobar v. Gonzales, 417 F.3d 363 (3d Cir. 2005) ("Honduran street children" not cognizable); Castillos Sanchez v. Attorney General, 523 F. App'x 682 (11th Cir. 2013) ("young males who are actively recruited by gangs because they have no father or other protective male in the home" not cognizable); Diaz Ruano v. Holder, 458 F. App'x 9 (1st Cir. 2012) ("young men targeted for recruitment by the criminal gangs in Guatemala" and "individuals opposed to the criminal gangs in Guatemala" not cognizable); Flores Munoz v. Holder, 2014 U.S. App. LEXIS 8974 (5th Cir. May 14, 2014) ("persons who resist gang membership" not cognizable); Galdamez v. Holder, 2014 U.S. App. LEXIS 3313 (5th Cir. 2014) ("young men who defy forced recruitment by the gangs in El Salvador" not cognizable); *Matter of* N-C-M-, 25 I. & N. Dec. 535 (BIA 2011) ("victims of gang violence" and "unwilling gang recruits" not cognizable); *Matter of* S-E-G-, 24 I. & N. Dec. 579 (BIA 2008) ("Salvadoran youth who have been subjected to recruitment efforts (continued...)

Holder, the First Circuit upheld the denial of asylum to an alien who claimed to fear persecution due to his membership in the group of "young Salvadoran men who have resisted gang recruitment and whose parents are unavailable to protect them."[113] The First Circuit did so, in part, because it found no evidence in the record suggesting that Salvadoran society viewed the purported group as a "discrete class of persons."[114] It also deferred to the BIA's view that the proposed grouping of "youths who resist gang recruitment" was "too subjective and open-ended" to meet the particularity requirement since it represented a "large, diffuse portion of society."[115] It gave similar deference to the BIA's view that "lack of parental protection" failed the "particularity" requirement, as there are no "objective criteria" to define what it means to lack parental protection.[116] The U.S. Court of Appeals for the Tenth Circuit relied upon similar logic in upholding the denial of asylum based on membership in the proposed social group of "El Salvadoran women between the ages of 12 and 25 who have resisted gang recruitment" in its 2012 decision in *Rivera-Barrientos v. Holder*.[117] There, the court opined that the proposed group could potentially be seen as possessing particularity, as the meaning of each of its terms is unambiguous.[118] However, it found that the group lacked social visibility (now social distinction) since there was no evidence that "women between the ages of 12 and 25 who have resisted gang recruitment are perceived to be a social group by Salvadoran society."[119]

These and other cases suggest that obtaining asylum based on membership in a group of persons targeted for, or resistant to, gang recruitment may be complicated by pervasiveness of gang violence in certain societies. Because the gangs are generally seen as targeting everyone who seems a likely candidate for membership, regardless of their personal attributes or associations, it can be hard to show that persons who have been targeted for or refused gang recruitment are seen as a discrete group by society.[120] It can also be hard to show that clear boundaries demarcate persons who have been targeted for or refused gang recruitment,[121] particularly since the BIA and the federal courts have generally taken the view that a particular social group cannot be defined "circularly" by the fact that its members have been targeted for persecution.[122]

(...continued)

by MS-13 and who have rejected or resisted membership in the gang based on their own personal, moral, and religious opposition to the gang's values and activities" not cognizable); *Matter of* E-A-G-, 24 I. & N. Dec. 591 (BIA 2007) ("persons resistant to gang membership" not cognizable).

[113] 675 F.3d 9, 11 (1st Cir. 2012).

[114] *Id.* at 14-16.

[115] *Id.* at 15.

[116] *Id.* at 17.

[117] 666 F.3d 641, 643 (9th Cir. 2012).

[118] *Id.* at 650.

[119] *Id.* at 653.

[120] *See, e.g., Mayorga-Vidal*, 675 F.3d at 16 (noting that the alien's situation, in being recruited by the gang, is "far from unique among Salvadoran children" in a country "swarming with unsupervised, uncared-for young people").

[121] *See, e.g., id.* (affirming the immigration judge's finding that the alien petitioner's proffered group is "too broad and encompasses too large a percentage of the population" to constitute a particular social group).

[122] *See, e.g., Rivera-Barrientos*, 666 F.3d at 651 ("Although a social group cannot be defined exclusively by the fact that its members have been subjected to harm ... this may be a relevant factor in considering the group's visibility in society.") (internal quotations omitted); *Solis-Gonzalez*, 523 F. App'x at 321 ("[A] social group may not be circularly defined by the fact that it suffers persecution.").

Former Gang Members

Granting asylum to aliens based on their membership in groups made up of former gang members is more complicated in that several federal courts of appeals have evidenced at least some willingness to view former gang members as a particular social group, while others have suggested that granting asylum to those who belong to organizations that have perpetrated acts of violence or other crimes in their home countries is contrary to the humanitarian purposes of asylum. For example, in its 2010 decision in *Urbina-Mejia v. Holder*, the Sixth Circuit found that being a member of a gang is a characteristic that is "impossible to change, except perhaps by rejoining the group."[123] The Seventh Circuit relied upon similar logic in its 2009 decision in *Benitez Ramos v. Holder*, finding that "[a] gang is a group, and being a former member of a group is a characteristic impossible to change."[124] However, neither decision took into account the social visibility (now, distinction) and particularity of the group in reaching this conclusion, and other tribunals have taken the opposite view. The Ninth Circuit, for example, has found that former gang members are categorically excluded from consideration as a particular social group on the grounds that recognizing former members of "violent criminal gangs" would "undermine the legislative purpose of the INA."[125] The First Circuit has similarly quoted, with apparent approval, the BIA's view that "[t]reating affiliation with a criminal organization as ... membership in a social group is inconsistent with the principles underlying the bars to asylum and withholding of removal based on criminal behavior,"[126] discussed below ("Bars to Asylum").

Whether a claim to asylum based on former gang membership succeeds may thus depend, in large part, upon the jurisdiction in which it is made. The BIA's decision in 2014 in *Matter of W-G-R-* could potentially also complicate matters. The alien in that case alleged membership in a particular social group made up of "former members of the Mara 18 gang in El Salvador who have renounced their gang membership."[127] In upholding the immigration judge's denial of asylum to the alien, the BIA left open the possibility of successful gang-related claims.[128] However, it suggested that, even when former membership is an immutable characteristic that defines a particular social group, the group will "often need to be further defined with respect to the duration or strength of the members' active participation in the activity and the recency of their active participation if it is to qualify as a particular social group."[129] It also emphasized that

---

[123] 597 F.3d 360, 366 (6th Cir. 2010). The Sixth Circuit did not address the "social visibility" requirement because neither the immigration judge nor the BIA applied it and, thus, the issue was not before the court on appeal. *Id.* at 367 n.3. *See also* Martinez v. Holder, 740 F.3d 902 (4th Cir. 2014) (finding that the BIA erred in holding that an alien's former gang membership was not an immutable characteristic of a particular social group, without addressing whether a purported group of former gang members possess social visibility and particularity).

[124] 589 F.3d 426, 429 (7th Cir. 2009). The Seventh Circuit noted that the government had also argued that the proposed group of former gang members was not socially visible. However, it had previously found that the BIA's "social visibility" requirement constituted an unreasonable interpretation of the *refugee* definition. *Id.* at 430.

[125] *Arteaga*, 511 F.3d at 945-946 ("We cannot conclude that Congress, in offering refugee protection for individuals facing potential persecution through social group status, intended to include violent street gangs who assault people and who traffic in drugs and commit theft."). *See also* Cantarero v. Holder, 734 F.3d 82, 86 (1st Cir. 2013) ("The BIA reasonably concluded that, in light of the manifest humanitarian purpose of the INA, Congress did not mean to grant asylum to those whose association with a criminal syndicate has caused them to run into danger.").

[126] Yokoyama v. Holder, No. 13-711 NAC, 2014 U.S. App. LEXIS 11915, at *5 (2d Cir., June 25, 2014) (quoting *Matter of* E-A-G-, 24 I. & N. Dec. 591, 596 (BIA 2007)).

[127] 26 I. & N. Dec. at 209.

[128] *Id.* at 222. *See also Matter of M-E-V-G-*, 26 I. & N. Dec. at 251 (emphasizing that there is no "blanket rejection of all factual scenarios involving gangs," and that "[s]ocial group determinations are made on a case-by-case basis").

[129] *Matter of W-G-R-*, 26 I. & N. Dec. at 222.

---

showing that a group of former gang members is socially distinct will require documentation about the treatment or status of former gang members in society, not just documentation about gangs, gang violence, and treatment of current gang members.[130]

Witnesses or Informants against Gangs

Witnesses and informants against gangs have also been recognized as comprising a particular social group in some cases, the most notable of which is arguably the decision by the *en banc* Ninth Circuit in 2013 in *Henriquiz-Rivas v. Holder*.[131] There, a majority of the Ninth Circuit reversed a BIA decision denying asylum to an alien who claimed to fear persecution on account of her membership in a group made up of "person[s] who testified in a criminal trial against members of a gang" in El Salvador.[132] The majority did so because it viewed the BIA's decision as inconsistent with *Matter of C-A-*, wherein the BIA had contrasted the lack of social visibility of noncriminal informants with the social visibility of "those who testify against cartel members."[133] The majority also suggested that the perception of the persecutor may matter more in determining the cognizability of particular social groups than that of society generally, since those who are persecuted are persecuted "precisely because the persecutor recognizes the object of his persecution."[134] This view—which is not shared by all other tribunals[135]—would seem to have informed the majority's approach insofar as gangs may well perceive persons who testify against them as a "group" even if the rest of society does not.

However, as Judge Kozinski's dissent in *Henriquiz-Rivas* illustrates, not all courts would necessarily adopt the view that witnesses against the gangs make up a particular social group.[136] Judge Kozinski's concerns centered upon the majority's reading of *Matter of C-A-* and, particularly, whether the BIA, in fact, found that witnesses are a cognizable social group in *Matter of C-A-*, or whether its statement contrasting witnesses with informants is best viewed as a nonbinding *dictum*.[137] He also noted that defining a particular social group based on its visibility to the persecutors runs the risk of defining the group circularly, based on the fact that its members have been subjected to harm.[138]

---

[130] *Id.* at 222, 225.

[131] 707 F.3d 1081 (9th Cir. 2013). *See also* Diane Uchimiya, *Falling through the Cracks: Gang Victims as Casualties in Current Asylum Jurisprudence*, 23 BERKELEY LA RAZA L.J. 109, 138 n.225 (noting case wherein the immigration judge recognized a particular social group consisting of family members of those who actively oppose gangs in El Salvador by agreeing to be prosecutorial witnesses without compensation).

[132] 707 F.3d at 1083.

[133] *Id.* at 1092 (quoting *Matter of C-A-*, 23 I. & N. Dec. at 960 ("[V]isibility is limited to those informants who are discovered because they appear as witnesses or otherwise come to the attention of cartel members.").

[134] *Id.* at 1089.

[135] *See, e.g., Mendez-Barrera*, 602 F.3d at 27 ("The relevant inquiry is whether the social group is visible in the society, not whether the alien herself is visible to the alleged persecutors."); *In re* A-M-E, 24 I. & N. Dec. 69, 74 (BIA 2007) (similar).

[136] *See also* Soriano v. Holder, 569 F.3d 1162 (9th Cir. 2009) (affirming the BIA's finding that "government informants" do not constitute a cognizable social group); Scatambuli v. Holder, 558 F.3d 53 (1st Cir. 2009) (persons who provided the U.S. government information about a smuggling ring not a cognizable group); *Matter of* C-A-, 23 I. & N. Dec. 951 (BIA 2006).

[137] 707 F.3d at 1102-1103.

[138] *Id.* at 1102 (arguing that "[d]efining a social group in terms of the perception of the persecutor risks finding that a group exists consisting of a persecutor's enemies list").

Other cases involving groups of witnesses or informants have failed on nexus grounds, because the persecutors are seen as motivated not by the alien's membership in a particular social group, but by personal retribution (see "On Account of").[139]

Family Members of Persons in the Foregoing Categories

Groups based on families were among the first social groups recognized by the BIA,[140] and family has since been described as a "prototypical example" of a particular social group.[141] In keeping with this view, some courts have been willing to consider the families of persons in some way affected by gang violence as a cognizable social group for purposes of asylum.[142] Other courts have been more skeptical.[143] Whether the group members share a common, immutable characteristic (i.e., family membership), and whether the group is defined with particularity, have generally not been at issue.[144] The requirement of social visibility (now social distinction), in contrast, has posed greater difficulties, since the family group must be one that is recognized as a discrete group.[145] Such recognition from the alien's society at large can be hard to come by unless the family in question is particularly famous or otherwise well known,[146] although it could

---

[139] *See* Amilcar-Orellana v. Mukasey, 551 F.3d 86 (1st Cir. 2008).

[140] *See, e.g., In re* H-, 21 I. & N. Dec. 337 (BIA 1996) (recognizing family membership in the Marehan subclan in Somalia as a social group); *Matter of Acosta*, 19 I. & N. Dec. at 232-233 ("A purely linguistic analysis of this ground of persecution [i.e., particular social group] suggests that it may encompass persecution seeking to punish either people in a certain relation, or having a certain degree of similarity, to one another or people of like class or kindred interests, such as shared ethnic, cultural, or linguistic origins, education, *family background*, or perhaps economic activity.") (emphasis added). The BIA subsequently dropped the focus upon persecution as "punishment" suggested here.

[141] *Sanchez-Trujillo*, 801 F.2d at 1576-1577.

[142] *See, e.g.*, Aldana-Ramos v. Holder, 757 F.3d 9 (1st Cir. 2014) (remanding the asylum claim to the BIA upon finding that the aliens' family could meet the criteria for membership in a particular social group); Crespin-Valladares v. Holder, 632 F.3d 117 (4th Cir. 2011) (family members of El Salvadoran citizens who actively opposed gangs by agreeing to be prosecutorial witnesses constitute a protected social group); *Lopez-Soto*, 383 F.3d at 235-236 (immigration judge accepting the immediate family as a particular social group); Molina-Estrada v. INS, 293 F.3d 1089, 1095 (9th Cir. 2002) (stating that family may constitute a particular social group in some circumstances); Martinez-Seren v. Holder, 394 F. App'x 404 (remanding to the BIA for consideration of the family as a particular social group); Elyse Wilkinson, *Examining the Board of Immigration Appeals' Social Visibility Requirement for Victims of Gang Violence Seeking Asylum*, 62 ME. L. REV. 387, 390 n.14 (noting a case where the immigration judge recognized as a particular social group a "subset of nuclear [] family at which MS 13 directed its persecution because [] (the respondent's brother) refused to join MS").

[143] *See, e.g.*, Bonilla-Morales v. Holder, 607 F.3d 1132 (6th Cir. 2010) (expressing doubt about a particular social group made up of family members of youth who have been subject to gang recruitment efforts, but not reaching the issue because the claim failed the "nexus" requirement); *Hernandez Tumacaj*, 535 F. App'x at 865-866 (BIA not required to address whether the alien's family constituted a particular social group where a "nexus" was found to be lacking); Perez-Perez v. Holder, No. 13-1711, 2014 U.S. App. LEXIS 8767 (4th Cir., May 9, 2014).

[144] *But see In re S-E-G-*, 24 I. & N. Dec. 579 at (rejecting family as a social group because it was not particular enough).

[145] *See, e.g., Constanza*, 647 F.3d at 753-754 (proposed social group of "family that experienced gang violence" not socially visible); *Ulloa Santos*, 552 F. App'x at 202 (remanding the case to the BIA for consideration of whether the persecution had a nexus to a protected ground, but not requiring reconsideration of the finding that the proposed social group of the alien's family lacked visibility). *See also* notes 134 and 138 and accompanying text (discussing whose perception of the group—that of the society at large or the persecutor—matters most).

[146] *See, e.g., Aldana-Ramos*, 757 F.3d at 22 ("There may be scenarios in which a wealthy family, targeted in part for its wealth, may still be the victims of persecution as a family. For instance, a local militia could single out a prominent wealthy family, kidnap family members for ransom, effectively drive the family into poverty, and pursue them throughout the country in order to show the local community that even its most prominent families are not immune and that the militia's rule must be respected.").

---

potentially be more easily shown when the focus is upon the perceptions of the alleged persecutor.[147]

A perceived lack of a "nexus" between the feared persecution and the alien's belonging to a particular family could also pose issues.[148]

Bars to Asylum

The INA also articulates certain bars to asylum, expressly prohibiting the executive branch from granting asylum to aliens who ordered, incited, assisted, or otherwise participated in the persecution of any person on account of race, religion, nationality, political opinion, or membership in a particular social group.[149] Also barred are aliens who may otherwise meet the requirements of the *refugee* definition, but (1) having been convicted of a "particularly serious crime," constitute a danger to the U.S. community; (2) committed a "serious nonpolitical crime" outside the United States prior to arriving here; (3) are reasonably believed to be a danger to U.S. security; (4) are inadmissible or deportable on certain terrorist grounds; or (5) were firmly resettled in another country prior to coming to the United States.[150] The INA further provides that aliens who have been convicted of "aggravated felonies"—which the INA defines to mean certain specified crimes (e.g., murder, rape, sexual abuse of a minor), as well as "crimes of violence" for which the term of imprisonment is at least one year[151]—are considered to have been convicted of particularly serious crimes.[152]

> **Time Bars on Applications for Asylum**
>
> In addition to the conduct-related bars noted here, Section 208 of the INA generally provides that aliens who cannot demonstrate by "clear and convincing evidence" that their application for asylum was filed within one year of their arrival in the United States are barred from seeking asylum. However, exceptions may be granted when the alien demonstrates, "to the satisfaction of [federal officials]" that there are changed circumstances which materially affect the alien's eligibility for asylum, or the delay in filing is related to "extraordinary circumstances."
>
> Congress has also provided that applications for asylum by unaccompanied alien children are not subject to this time bar.
>
> *See generally* INA §208(a)(1)(B)& (D), 8 U.S.C. §1158(a)(1)(B)& (D).

These bars can present potentially significant issues for former gang members, as to whom there could be "serious reasons" to believe they have committed "serious nonpolitical crimes" outside

---

[147] Having family members who remain in the country could also pose issues for claims to asylum based on membership in a particular social group made up of a family. *See, e.g., Santos-Lemus*, 542 F.3d at 743 ("Santos-Lemus's mother's continuing safety in El Salvador is substantial evidence supporting the Board's finding that Santos-Lemus does not have a well-founded fear of future persecution. We have considered the continuing safety of family members to be an important factor in determining whether a petitioner has a well-founded fear of future persecution.").

[148] *See, e.g.*, de Abarca v. Holder, No. 13-1081, 2014 U.S. App. LEXIS 13020 (1st Cir. 2014) (upholding the denial of asylum).

[149] As previously noted, those who have engaged in persecution are expressly excluded from the definition of *refugee*. *See supra* note 13 and accompanying text.

[150] INA §208(b)(2)(A)(i)-(vi), 8 U.S.C. §1158(b)(2)(A)(i)-(vi).

[151] INA §101(a)(42), 8 U.S.C. §1101(a)(42).

[152] INA §208(b)(2)(B)(i), 8 U.S.C. §1158(b)(2)(B)(i).

the United States.[153] Those who are not former gang members are generally less likely to be affected by such bars.

Author Contact Information

Kate M. Manuel
Legislative Attorney
kmanuel@crs.loc.gov, 7-4477

---

[153] *See, e.g.*, Ramos v. Holder, 589 F.3d 426, 431 (7th Cir. 2009) ("Ramos was a member of a violent criminal group for nine years. If he is found to have committed violent acts while a member of the gang (as apparently he did, although the evidence is not entirely clear), he may be barred from the relief he seeks for reasons unrelated to whether he is a member of a 'particular social group'."); *Examining the Board of Immigration Appeals' Social Visibility Requirement, supra* note 142, at 396-397 (describing the bar on aliens who have committed serious crimes as "making it nearly impossible for ex-gang members to be granted asylum"). Some have suggested, however, that the young age at which a child joined a gang, or his or her having been "forced" to do so, should be taken into consideration when considering the applicability of the bars to asylum and refugee status to former gang members. *See, e.g.*, UNHCR, Guidelines on International Protection: Child Asylum Claims under Articles 1(A)2 and 1(F) of the 1951 Convention and/or 1967 Protocol Relating to the Status of Refugees, Dec. 22, 2009, *available at* http://www.refworld.org/docid/4b2f4f6d2.html. *See also* Negusie v. Holder, 555 U.S. 511 (2009) (whether the alien was coerced to persecute must be considered in determining whether the "persecutor bar" to asylum applies).